Dedication

This true story is dedicated to all men and women who served and are serving our country, especially those who have made the extreme sacrifice, their lives. Also to those who suffered or who are suffering mental and physical disabilities. A special thanks to the following individuals, who have generously helped to tell this true story my beloved wife Helen, radioman Ross Mergenthaler and Vietnam Veteran Jerry Koppes

Acknowledgements

I would like to extend my appreciation to the following for photographs used in the book. Radar Man Joe Duban, Timothy Aanerud, Larry Smith, Tim Adams, Josh Curtis, Warren Thompson, Ken Rust, and Norman Taylor, authors; Robert F. Dorr, John Pimbolt, Chester Marshall and Glenn E. McClure. Also the AAF, Army, and US Navy. I also want to thank authors Raymond Clampon and Allan Ede for their shared expertise.

ISBN-10: 069-201-855-7

ISBN-13: 978-069-201-855-2

Self Published: August 2012

The Author

Edward Francis Heiberger

Ed Heiberger

Contents

Chapter I
Boyhood Days

Sadly my dad died when I was six years old. I had three older sisters; Bertille, Laura, Anna Mae also an older brother Raymond who later served in World War II in the tank corps in Germany. My mom had us five kids in grade school to raise, tough, but she did it. It was the Great Depression years in the mid-30s, a struggle for most people. For entertainment the neighborhood boys would get together and we played football, with a rolled up sock.

The grade school that I attended had the order of St. Francis nuns who were very strict. If you got out of line you had to hold out your hand to get wacked by a ruler. We would clench and pull our hands back. One time the nun held out my hand, but I still yanked it back and she wacked her knuckles really hard, which proved to be quite painful.

A student who sat in front of me was Jack Schueller and one time he turned around and gave me a box with the words "world's smallest musical instrument" on it. I couldn't imagine what it was. So I opened it and there was a bean.

The school held a bazaar in the church basement. Jerry Finkenhauer, Otto Berwanger, Paul Meyers, and I put on a skit to help raise money. We put on dresses and black faces and pretended we did laundry. It was all made up as we went along. Some skits were 2 minutes long and others were 5 minutes long. The kids really lined up with their pennies and it was a huge, huge, success!

Two of my closest buddies were Paul Meyers and Otto Berwanger. We often swiped fruit from various neighbors. We would get cherries, apples, plums, grapes, pears, and even strawberries. One day we were walking about a block from my home and a lady came out of her house and said "If you boys go get me some cherries, I will make you a cherry pie" Wow, oh boy! We got her a lot of cherries; it was the best pie I ever ate! Then on one occasion we went to swipe grapes at night. We were in the vineyard when Paul turned on a flashlight. I said "What the hell are you doing, trying to get us caught?" He said, "Hey, I've got to see if they are ripe"

The handyman whose name was Jim worked for the Rhomberg Fur Company at their residence and once in a while he treated kids to an ice cream cone. It was really a nice thing to do, however, being kids, we still swiped apples there at the Rhomberg's.

It was very seldom that I got to make a trip to the butcher shop to buy a pound of hamburger. The butcher would give me a piece of ham sausage, a really great treat for me.

A real bonanza was when Paul and Otto found out a person could go to the bakery at 5 am with a nickel and a flour sack and get it filled up with day old bakery goods. We would get a large variety of doughnuts, jelly rolls, small pies, cinnamon rolls, Twinkies, etc. My mother was really happy when I came home with all this good food. It was sure a welcomed addition to feed us at our table.

In those early years we had ice boxes. The ice man would carry in 25 pounds, 50 pounds, 75 pounds to 100 pounds into houses. I had to be sure to empty the large pan under the ice box before the water overflowed, otherwise my mother would really get upset. While he was delivering, we kids would eat ice chips off the wagon. It is sure a wonder we didn't get sick.

The neighbor lady, Mrs. May, would get as many as 17of us kids together and give us a long ride to the Municipal Public Swimming Pool in her Mercury in the summer time. We also had to hang on the running boards and fenders. Luckily she never got stopped for overloading. The car was really weighted down, but we all got there safely. We really appreciated the ride.

In the winter I had clamp-on ice skates and a hand me down sleigh. One wintry day, after a fresh snow fall, I was outside alone when the milk man and his 2 horse drawn wagon came along. The horses automatically stopped along the way and he carried his wire case with several bottles to customers. I still don't know what prompted me, but I started to throw snow on the horses backs. Soon they stampeded off down the street with the milk man hollering after them yelling "Whoa, whoa, whoa" as they ran out of sight.

A couple of weeks later there was about a six inch snowfall. We could easily pack it into a snowball. Six seventh graders got together in an early evening and filled a neighbor friend Jack Kasel's front porch with three foot snowballs so you couldn't open the front door. We just had to be mischievous.

Usually it was Otto and I who went to play with the neighbor friend, Jack Kasel. We always ended up teasing him mercilessly. His mother would come out and say, "I'm calling your mother, Eddie Heiberger!" and she did. My mother would get a switch off the bush and wail on my behind. Finally, I got tired of this and said to Otto, "I'm not going to Jack's any more, she always calls my mother." Otto said, "Well if she does it again, I will just tell her 'Why don't you call my mother?'" Sure enough, she was again going to call my mother and Otto said, "Why don't you call my mother?" and she did. Otto really got it and he said that it was the last time he would ever try to do that again.

A few of my jobs around the house were cleaning out the garage, trimming the hedge, cutting the grass, snow shoveling, and sprinkling ashes on the side walk when it was icy in the winter, and in the spring taking out the large living room carpet and beating it with a wire beater. I pretended it was a baseball bat and I raised clouds of dust. I also had to throw the kindling wood into the basement window when it got dumped by the truck in the alley. This was usually about once a year. I had to do it really fast as it blocked the alley and I had to get finished before a car came along.

A 10-year-old neighbor boy, Bob Howes, lived across the street from me and got a new BB gun. At the time I was eight years old. There was a shed with a window with six sections of glass in it setting about 100 feet from the front sidewalk. We took turns to see if we could hit one of the windows. Nothing happened, we shot and shot and couldn't understand why the glass didn't break. Finally we walked to the shed and all the windows had BB holes in them. My mom paid for the glass and his dad installed them. I really caught hell for that!

I had a Des Moines Register Sunday paper route which was over a mile long. Rain, snow or sleet, I had to pick up papers at four o'clock in the morning on 24th Street at the bus barn. I had to use a sled or a wagon or bike if weather permitted. The papers were too heavy to carry. I was glad when I would make it back home. I wanted a bicycle real bad, and figured if I saved fifty cents a week for a year I could buy one. My route paid me 62 cents a week. I had to deliver on Sundays, collect the money on Mondays and Tuesdays, and then pay for the papers on Wednesdays. One year later, I had a shiny new bicycle.

When I was about 14, I worked for the Artesian Bottling Company, a soda water factory. In December of 1941, the owner, Mr. Shanahan said, "you will be just like me, too young for this war and too old for the next." Boy was he ever wrong!

In the summer it was a lot of swimming and baseball and fishing. One day I went fishing by myself in the Mississippi, there were a lot of people fishing along the bank. I was sixteen at the time, the age you had to have a fishing license, which I did not have. Along came the game warden checking licenses. He really caught me off guard; he asked me what year I was born. I answered, "1925", and he left. I realized I made myself a year older, instead of saying 1927, making myself a year younger. I grabbed my gear and beated out of there as fast as I could.

One day when I was 16, five of us guys on three bicycles took a ride up to the Eagle Point Park in Dubuque, IA. We horsed around the park for a little while and soon three girls came around. They were about twenty years old and they started flirting with us. I guess they thought it would be fun. After a few hours, we were going to leave. They asked for a ride down the hill and we said, "sure!"

The hill was a very curvy, steep grade and quite long. Cy Stierman took the lead with Bob Duehr on the back and Rita Schadel sitting on the bar in front of Cy. At the bottom of the hill there was a very sharp turn with a cement railing on each side. Cy's brakes would not work and he smashed into the cement railing, Rita got a broken leg.

Then a car came from the long way down, saw the accident and the driver stopped in the middle of the street to lend assistance. Then my first cousin Bert Stierman came down with Bill Giese on the back and a girl name Lois on the bar in front. He crashed into the back of the car and Lois got a fractured skull. Bert said that his brakes failed, but he could have made the turn if the car wasn't there. Then I came down with just the girl on the bar. I just stopped at the bottom. The next day I took my bike and was going to go down a hill and thought I better be sure my brakes work. They didn't, so I got them replaced right away.

At Senior High School, I had the lead in the senior class play, 'Ever Since Eve'. My buddy in the play was Arthur Zahler who never memorized his lines. The drama coach, Edra Walters told him a couple days before the play was to go on "We are not going to put this play on at all if you are not going to learn your lines." Arthur said, "Well I always know my lines, and I will know them on the night of the play for sure!" So we did put on the play.

Well, during the play, at one point I was to reach for Susan, the girl in the play, like I was going to kiss her when a cop was to knock at the door and I was to step back. During the play the cop did not knock at the door at the correct time and I practically fell into her. Then good ole Arthur didn't know his lines, so I said a few lines back again so he could pick up on it and he looked at me and said, "You said that before!"

Then the three of us are sitting on the couch, Arthur, Joan Phillips in the middle, and me. She wore a strapless evening gown except for two very small straps. She is crying in the play and we each took turns comforting her, reaching behind her back putting her head on our shoulders. One time I accidentally brushed the strap off and it drooped down around her arm. Arthur looked at me and said, "Shame on you, shame on you!"

At 17, I did graduate from Senior High school. The summer of '43 went by very quickly. During that time I worked in a grocery store to earn some extra money. In the fall I enrolled at Loras College. A couple friends of mine; Joe Stieber, Spook Maloney and I had a ball. I never heard how Spook got his nick name. Anyhow, we went out on dates, went to dances at Melody Mill, and even though at just seventeen, we went to the night clubs in East Dubuque, IL. We could buy liquor there, even though we were under the legal age limit.

Spook's folks owned a cottage about six miles north of Dubuque. We had a few good hell raising parties there also. At the college, for a diversion, we would get together at the book store and see who could throw pennies closest to the wall. After completion of my first semester and into the start of my second, I got called into active duty in the Army Air Force on February 22, 1944. Upon completion of service, years later, I did graduate from college.

Paul   Otto   Me (author)

We got into plenty of mischief.

Jack Kasel

Friend, classmate and neighbor.
Often the target of pranks.

Proudly sitting on my shiny new bicycle.

CHAMPIONS OF BOYS' CLUB LEAGUES

Title winners in the Junior Boys' League were the Termites. Left to right, they are: Front—Eddie Blaser, Co-Captain Don Breitbach, Eddie Heiberger, and Carl Striblow. Rear—Coach John Hoyman, Rob Schlueter, Herbie Herber, Co-Captain Rich Jahn, Bob Jacobi, and Paul Weiss.

The house I was born and raised.
My mom's in the picture.

My Senior High School graduation picture.

Chapter II
Army Air Force Stateside Service

It began on a nice wintry day in December of 1943 at the Dubuque Municipal Airport. Airplane rides were being given in a Piper Cub, a small single-winged plane, for those who might be interested in the Army Air Force. I was 17 and did not like the thought of someone possibly running at me with a bayonet or sleeping in the mud or snow for the Army. Also I wasn't a good swimmer, so that ruled out the Navy for me.

Two of my buddies watched as I climbed in and a got short ride once around above the airfield. I climbed out and said, "That wasn't bad at all, that is for me." So the three of us; Stan Cook, Bill Parr, and I enlisted at Camp Dodge, in Des Moines, IA on January 26, 1944. My mother could hardly believe this as I didn't like to get on a six foot step ladder.

We had a big pillow fight in the hotel, and then got our shots. While in line, a fellow a few ahead of me passed out. They dragged him to a chair and jabbed him in each arm, seemed brutal to me at the time. We got a physical and were issued our uniforms. We were herded through pretty fast. I was really surprised when the corporal said, "Your left shoulder is higher than your right." We were now in the First Air Force, later I was assigned to the Second and finally to the 20th Air Force.

Then on February 22, 1944, we were all put on a train to go from Des Moines, IA to Biloxi, Mississippi. Volunteers passed out free cigarettes. I played my first poker game on the train, a five and ten cent game and couldn't believe I won $30. It was sure a lot of fun. As we passed through the towns the people were out for us, waving and cheering. A lot of kids kept running alongside the train. Upon arrival we were put on trucks to go into the camp. It was late at night and the lights were dim. It looked pretty darn dreary in the camp. A few soldiers hollered out, "You'll be sorry!" and we were, but of course we hollered the same thing to the next group of guys.

I got stuck with KP. I was dishing out large gobs of jello to each soldier, until a corporal came along, I only gave him half as much and he complained. I turned to Don Heitzman, wearing a white coat, he was just a private like me, and said "Sergeant Heitzman, this corporal won't move along and you told me to cut down on the jello." He said, "Move along corporal", and I then proceeded to give out large gobs. I grinned at the guy next to me because I got away with it.

I was told never to volunteer. One day after a drill we were sitting on the ground and the sergeant said that he needed volunteers to do some labor work. Those that don't volunteer will have it a lot rougher here. And we all just sat around the rest of the day. I couldn't believe my luck. Then a lieutenant gave us a talk. The one thing that he said that always stuck in my mind was "You can get anything you want if you know how to talk." I imagine practice would make perfect.

We were all issued sewing kits but most of us weren't very skilled. We went into Gulfport and had our air force patches and the braid around our caps sewed on by professionals.

During our stay at Biloxi, Mississippi, we fired a forty-five pistol, a carbine, which could be drawn as fast as a pistol, a sub machine gun called "The Grease Gun" and an M-1 rifle. They also listed me as a reserve bombadier after trying to follow a spot around on a phonograph.

The sergeant gathered about 40 of us together one day for a gas mask drill. He had us put on the gas mask and go into a building filled with tear gas. Then inside, we had to take the gas mask off and run outside, tears streaming down our faces. Next he had us sitting on a small knoll with our gas masks put away in their cases. He set off mustard gas, highly poisonous, about thirty yards away. It was yellow, and suddenly the wind shifted and it blew towards us. Everybody ran, nobody tried to put on a gas mask!

We were told on a few occasions to prepare for inspection with foot lockers open. Everything had to be in order and the inspector came in with white gloves checking for dust. He would occasionally bounce a quarter off the bunk to see if the blankets were tight enough. Hell, I wasn't even in West Point and they were sure giving one hell of an inspection.

At five o'clock in the morning, when you had to get in formation, you had to have gloves on if it was cold. No gloves on hands or in pockets to keep warm, you would get a gig. A gig is a disciplinary mark on your personal record. The tests of physical fitness we had to do were chin-ups, push-ups, and sit-ups. The only one I excelled at were sit-ups, I could do a hundred.

The permanent party soldiers at Biloxi wore a pin on their caps. One day, I walked towards three of them. The sun was glistening off of the pins. I thought they were all officers and I snapped a salute. They really laughed and I felt about 2 inches high.

One of the airman's hygiene was very bad so we just told him to put his shoes outside and to take a good shower or we would give him one. Then there was another airman who was a big bragger. When he was gone, we tied strings from his springs to the cot. When he came in, he flopped on his cot and cracked his butt onto the floor.

In the barracks one day I heard one guy comment, "God, I just had KP three days ago and I am on for tomorrow". Don Heitzman said, "Why don't you go to the chaplain and get your tough situation card punched?"

Then when on KP one time the corporal said, "Is there a Ed Heiberger here?" He told me I had burned up my mattress. The entire group on KP gathered around to listen. I said, "I don't smoke", which I didn't at the time. He said, "Well, some sergeant probably burned up his own mattress, and put it on your bunk." He also told me it would take six months to pay for it and I would be lucky if I could buy soap and toothpaste. He told me to go on over to headquarters and they would take care of me.

I went over there and all I had to do was sign the payroll. Needless to say, I came back to the corporal and he said, "Don't feel bad, they used to tell me that I was shipping out, I would get all packed up and it would be a false alarm".

Sergeant Boss, the drill sergeant, got drunk a lot at night. He would come into our barracks, grab two cots at a time and dump us out in the middle of the night.

I had learned the Queen Anne salute, which involved twirling the rifle a lot. I was twirling away and the sergeant got in my face and said, "If you drop that rifle you will clean every rifle in this platoon." You know, kind of as a gutsy teenager at the time, I kept twirling. Lucky, I never dropped it.

There was one soldier standing in front of a mirror, dressed in a Class A uniform, combing his hair, getting ready to go to town. I said there is no doubt why he is called 'slick'. You could grease a two ton truck with what he puts on his hair.

I got stuck at headquarters to run errands riding a bicycle. They sent me on one errand after another. I peddled as fast as I could figuring I would get caught up and could take it easy. Finally I was all wore out, when the guy asked me to go to the PX and bring him 2 candy bars. I blew up and said, "I may have to run regular errands, but I don't have to run your personal errands". Listen to this! Then he says, "You did enough, go bring four guys to take your place" the gall! Four guys to replace me! I went to a barracks where nobody knew me, I pointed to four guys and said, "I need four guys to volunteer, you and you and you and you."

Down there in Biloxi, the sun was always shining and you always had your rain coat with you because it could just start raining out of the blue. We went on a fifteen mile hike and had to carry a full pack that weighed about forty pounds. When we got there we dug a little trench around the tent to keep the water out. Then it rained buckets of water accompanied by the fiercest lightning.

It struck right in our midst. One guy was out with a shovel digging his trench and it killed him. Another guy was struck blind. You would pull back a tent flap and the guys would be unconscious with their eyes rolled back into their head. It just woke me up, knocking me about three to four feet into the air. The lieutenant in charge just cursed and hollered and screamed and screamed and screamed to send every available ambulance, which they finally did. Many men were offered discharges.

That night one of the guys went to the PX for a candy bar. On his way back the lightning started again. He came in just shaking like a leaf. But, when we were on hikes there was always just one ambulance along. The fellows who had badly hurt feet or were suffering from heat exhaustion would get a ride in the ambulance; we called it the meat wagon.

In the barracks when somebody would take a nap, there was usually someone around who would give him a hot foot. One day I took a nap and get this, they used a wood match and stuck the head of the match into my shoe. I was exhausted, that match burned all the way down, flared up and went out. I woke up with a lot of pain and hollered, "Who did it?" with my fists clenched. It was clear I would take on anybody. But there were no takers. At that time I weighed a mere 140 pounds. I was probably lucky there were no takers!

We arrived in Denver May 1, 1944. To our surprise, shortly after our arrival, it snowed there and we were actually issued boots. We were there for training for remote control turrets and also had to disassemble and reassemble a fifty caliber machine gun.

While at Denver I met a very beautiful girl roller skating, probably 18 or 19 years old. I asked her out and she said, "I was married once and engaged twice." I said "If it doesn't bother you, it doesn't bother me". We did date a few times. On the dates that I had we would usually catch a movie, stroll through town or a path and end the date with a pleasant kiss.

Back in basic training, we did a lot of marching. I could practically count the hairs on the back of Al Kovac's neck. Al and I had a lot of fun at Danceland, a dance hall located in a building upstairs. We danced with different partners all night long.

In downtown Denver there was a large pond. We got a passerby to take a picture of me holding Al Kovac over the pond. I darn near dropped him and he thought for sure he was going to get dunked.

I had lost 11 pounds in basic training, but the food was so good in Denver that I gained 23 pounds. When you went down the chow line and came to the slabs of ice cream, you were allowed one. Almost every guy tried to get two. They had one guy on KP whose job it was to allow only one and if you tried to get a second, he would jab you in the hand with a fork. You had to be fast to avoid the fork.

It was about this time when I met Frank B. Giles. Whenever we got up to start to drill, here was this guy in our barrack with a Class A, dress uniform on suntans. One day I asked him, "How come we drill and you wear a Class A uniform?" He said, "I just tell them I am going on sick call". So...I started hanging around with Frank. Frank and I ended up on KP one day, they called out various jobs and you could take what you wanted. You just volunteered.

They asked who wanted to wash trays. I said, "Let's do it", Frank said, "No". They asked who wanted to scrub the floor, I said, "Ok", Frank said, "No". And then an easy one came out, lining up bottles of salt and so forth on the tables. I said, "That's us", Frank said, "No way." Then garbage detail. I shut my mouth, but Frank said, "That's us". We carried out four garbage cans and ate ice cream all day from the kitchen!

Another time we got caught doing something or another, the Sergeant took us to a furnace room about 14 feet by 30 feet and said, "I want this to be so clean I can eat off of it when I get back, which will be exactly at 1600 hours." I told Frank, "We better get busy, that sergeant was really mad!" Frank said, "Sit down, and take it easy, no hurry." Then about a half an hour before he was due back we just soaked the mops and spilled buckets of water all over the floor. Sergeant came back in and took a look around and said, "Nice job boys!"

The sergeant had the whole platoon together to police the area. That is picking up everything, like the cigarette butts that were all over the place. You had to field strip them, in other words, roll the paper into a small ball, throw it away, and scatter the tobacco into the wind. The Sergeant said, "All I want to see is elbows and ass holes" Frank says, "Follow me", so we go picking up around the corner of the building out of sight. Frank says, "Let's go to the PX and get a malt!" I said, "geez" but we did. We finished, came back around the building picking up like nothing had happened.

Another time in Denver, Bert Jones, real nice, quiet guy, was planning on getting married as soon as the war was over. He could play the piano as good as Liberace. One piece that I really liked, I still like it to this day was "Whispering". I would always ask him to play that, and he always played it for me, and I really enjoyed that.

Pepi, Miller, Parent, and I were browsing in a downtown store in Denver one day. A woman came up to us and said, "Oh, isn't that a cute mascot you have there" she was referring to our tail gunner who was very short and looked very young for his age. Boy was he really steaming. I don't blame him for getting mad.

While we were in Denver, seven of us fellows got together and rented a car and traveled to Colorado Springs and saw Garden of the Gods, Cave of the Winds, and Red Rock. It was really a nice relief from our regular routine.

Then when we would be marching along, a couple things we would sing were "The second lieutenants will win the war, so what in the hell are we fighting for" and "We don't smoke, we don't chew, we don't go with the girls that do" as well as "Round her leg she wore a yellow ribbon".

While in Denver many times there wasn't a sergeant around to take us to chow. The rule was you had to go to chow in formation. The different fellows including myself played sergeant once in a while and called, "Fall in", "Attention", "Left right, left right, left right" on to the mess hall. That worked out pretty good.

The night we graduated from central fire control school, we were all in our bunks about asleep when two guys grabbed a third guy and stuck him under the shower. In the process it was a struggle and they all got wet, so they went after the fourth guy and naturally he joined in. Now there were four guys grabbing one guy and it snow balled. When they got to me, there was about ten. I fought like hell, but to no avail I joined in getting the next guy.

Again there were thousands of guys at the base in Denver. At the post office, I asked the girl for my mail and gave her my name. About a week or so later, I went back, but before I said anything she said, "There is no mail for you" I was astounded, she had a photographic memory.

While we were in Denver we had strict orders, whether we were on or off the base, as far as never saying a word about training on a B-29. We had to watch that pretty close. The next thing while at Denver, I had a nine day delay in route to travel home first. The trains were jammed. I was in line quite a ways back. The conductor stopped the line about ten guys in front of me saying that the train was full. The guy in front of me said to the conductor, "My buddy got on there", and the conductor said, "Go on ahead". So then I piped up and said, "Mine got on there too", and the conductor let me get on too. I never had a buddy getting on. The train went to Davenport, IA, and I hitch hiked to Dubuque, IA.

I will never forget when I reached the city limits. A woman called out to me from her porch and asked if I wanted some breakfast, I declined but asked her to call me a cab. My time at home on the ten day delay en route raced by. Most of my friends were in the service, I was really glad to see mom and my sisters. I went to a few bars and a couple of dances. Before I knew it, it was time to head to Clovis, New Mexico.

On August 28, 1944 we arrived in Clovis, New Mexico for training flights. We took one training flight on a B-17 bomber and the rest were on a B-29.

At Clovis we were issued our flight suits and jackets. It was quite a thrill, especially the first time rumbling down the runway to take off wondering if this gigantic plane could get off the ground. On training missions on Friday nights, we could look down and see those postage sized fields in the various cities lit up for their Friday night football games. These were generally peaceful flights.

Again there were thousands of soldiers on the base there. There were girls that worked at the PX and sold various items. But the chance to take a girl out was very slim. I asked a girl at the cigarette counter about going out, no dice. So I walked around a bit and thought what a stranger I was, so I went back and talked to her for about 30 minutes, then asked if I could walk her home, she accepted. Later, I dated her a time or two. It was nice to talk to a member of the opposite sex.

Portales, Mexico was just 19 miles away. We would hitch hike back and forth on Friday nights. One night three of us left the dance a little late and had a hell of a time getting a ride back. The car traffic was practically nothing. We thought it was funny that we might be called AWOL, and couldn't stop laughing. But we actually did make it back on time. At Clovis, we received our oversea shots.

One of my buddies there was married and said that his wife was coming. Why don't I take out the girl that he was going with Joan Breech from Portales, New Mexico. So I got a date with her and upon my arrival she said that her parents were not home and asked if I would like to dance. So we were dancing and all of a sudden she looked up at me and said, "You are not very sexy are you?" My mouth really dropped wide open and I just kept on dancing. You know Miller, our left gunner, at one time said he had wished he had never slept with a woman before he got married. Personally I thought it was good advice.

Our crew was formed there. The following are the crew members and some statistics about them.

William Standen, Pilot, age 25 from Idaho.

Murray Taylor, Co-pilot, age 24 from Washington.

Herman Copeland, Navigator, age 21 from California.

William Trotter, Bombadier, age 20 from New York.

Carl Taschinger, Flight Engineer, age 26 from Missouri.

Joseph Duban, Radar Man, age 19 from Pennsylvania.

Ross Mergenthaler, Radio Operator, age 21 from Ohio.

Edward Heiberger, Gun Commander, age 18 from Iowa.

John Miller, Left Gunner, age 23 from Massachusetts.

Louis Pepi, Right Gunner, age 19 from Massachusetts.

Edgar Parent, Tail Gunner, age 19 from Maine.

My official job description on the B-29 was Central Fire Control, but I was also referred to as Ring Gunner, Gun Commander and Top Gunner.

For the first four missions we had Murray Taylor flying with us as a co-pilot, he was then replaced by Jesse Chambers. We of course got really close up to a B-29. We were still commenting, "Look at the size of that, how can it get off the ground?" It was incredible.

On a training mission in a B-29, you had to fire 200 rounds of air to air gunnery before you were allowed to go overseas. The tow plane had some trouble, I don't know if the gunners hit the towing plane instead of the towing target, but it was not available. So each gunner had to fire 200 rounds off into space to qualify to go overseas. We did it.

While we were on this training mission the computer for the gunnery system caught on fire, and smoke filled the pilot compartment. We were told to get ready to bail out when we heard the bell. The pilot however managed to land safely without having to ring the bell. We scurried out at the landing and the fire was put out.

Another training flight, upon taking off, the plane started filling with gas fumes. A gas line had broken. The pilot had to cut the engines, but he managed to brake before the end of the runway.

Four of us gunners traveled to Albuquerque, New Mexico where we rented a hotel room. Eddie Parent, the tail gunner, called room service and told them to send up a bottle of whiskey. Parent expected it to be four or five dollars. The bell hop knocked at the door and handed the bottle to Parent. Parent set the bottle next to the door and reached for his wallet. The bellhop said, "17 dollars" Parent without a word shoved the bottle into the guy's chest and slammed the door in his face.

In Clovis, rarely, but it did happen, medical personnel would get everyone out of their sacks at about two o'clock in the morning for a medical check.

We arrived November 2, 1944 in Kearney, Nebraska, which was a staging area, awaiting the time to go overseas. While there we played some basketball. The four of us gunners went on into town and got a couple bottles of Virginia Dare wine. Then we went to the USO for paper cups for the "soda" we had outside to drink and then went to a movie. On the screen a man with a flashlight was looking at tombs. Our right gunner kicked over an empty bottle of wine, the bottle went "clink, clink" without breaking on the cement floor. He held up his lit lighter yelling, "Where is he, where is he?" That's when we got kicked out and that is when the wine hit me.

The three of us went walking down slowly to where a car was parked with girls in it. I tried unsuccessfully to climb into the back seat. Then I walked into a restaurant and sat on a stool with my head drooping. The manager said, "They sent the MPs after you", I said, "I don't care if they send all the MPs in the world after me". Two nice soldiers said they would help me onto the bus, and they did. Everybody had to get off the bus so it could be searched before entering the camp. They left me on the bus! I managed to fall into my bunk and closed my eyes. Someone tapped me on the shoulder and said, "Guard duty".

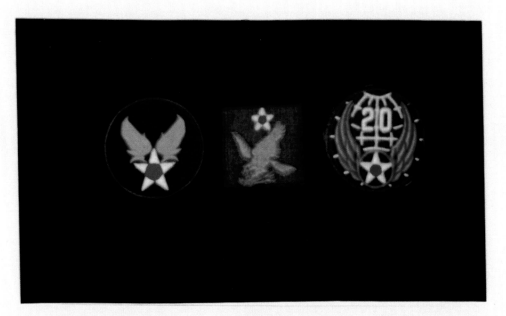

1ˢᵗ Air Force	2ⁿᵈ Air Force	20ᵗʰ Air Force

1st Air Force   2nd Air Force   20th Air Force

I was assigned to all three.

I almost dropped Al for a good dunking!

Cave of Winds.

Top Row, left to right

Al Kovac – Kansas City, Kansas
Richard Little – Lafayette, Indiana
George Hanson – Williamsburg, Iowa
Eugene Mount – Terra Haute, Indiana

Bottom row, left to right

Leonard Freidel – Lesterville, So. Dakota
Henry Stash – Chicago, Illinois
Ed Heiberger – Dubuque, Iowa

Delay en route. At home with mother, three sisters, and baby girl, Susan.

1st Lt. William G. Standen, AC 2. 1st Lt. Jess Chambers, Jr., Pilo[...]
[1]st Lt. Herman F. Copeland, Jr., Nav 4. 2nd Lt. William A Trotter, [...]
T/Sgt. Carl B. Tachinger, Flt/Eng 6. S/Sgt. Joseph J. Duban, Rad[...]
[...] Ross H. Mergenthaler, Radio 8. S/Sgt. Edward F. Heiberger, Rin[...]
[...] S/Sgt. John E. Miller, Lft Gunr 10. S/Sgt. Louis A. Pepi, Rgt Gu[...]
11. S/Sgt. Edgar S. Parent, Tail Gunr
[...]en   Z Square 54

Lt. Standen's crew picture on June 12, 1945 "Official
Picture from the 500th Bomb Group." Number 2, Jess
Chambers, flew as our co-pilot after our first four missions.

Chapter III
Overseas Combat Missions

Location: Mather Field, Sacramento, CA on November 22, 1944. We left on November 29, 1944 flying a new B-29 to Oahu, saw Honolulu, Pearl Harbor, on to Kwajelin, to Saipan. It was a long, tedious flight with thoughts of what lies ahead. The awesome B-29 Superfortress, the wing span was one hundred forty-one feet, ninety-nine feet in length and was twenty nine feet high. It was powered by four 2,200 horse power turbo charged, radial piston engines and fueled by 7,000 gallons of gasoline. The propellers were four bladed having a diameter of nearly 17 feet. It had three pressurized compartments, two forward ones were connected by a tunnel and the third was the tail gunner's. The armament consisted of four remote controlled turrets and a tail turret, with twelve 50 caliber machine guns and one 20 millimeter cannon loaded with 7500 rounds of ammunition. The price tag was over one million dollars.

Upon arrival at Saipan on December 3, 1944, our flight crew was assigned to the 73rd bomb wing, 500th bombardment group, the 883rd squadron. Everything was pretty well set up when we came. The construction of the airfield on Saipan was a huge task to accommodate B-29's. Thanks to the hard working Seabees. The Quonset huts were all built and in place, the mail room, the showers, the post office, the mess hall, and the theater under construction.

An officer sat down with us and gave us an orientation as to where the buildings were located and what to expect as we were going on our flights, our bombing missions. The one thing that he warned us strictly about was that whenever there was an air raid, to be sure to wear our shoes, because our feet would get cut by coral rock.

We were issued flak suits and helmets. When I tried on my flak helmet the first time, I found it to be too confining. I practically had to wedge my head up into the cramped space. It seems I had about a ¼ inch on each side. Therefore I never ever wore the flak helmet, I needed some head movement.

That night we were awakened from a sound sleep, an air raid. Nobody grabbed anything, we ran out cutting our feet on the coral rock. A Japanese plane was in our sight as we were looking out our fox hole coming towards us. We were all standing up looking at it. All of a sudden he opened fire and our heads went down like they were all on a string.

One Jap pilot got shot between the eyes after his plane crashed. Somehow, they seemed to be alive after they got out of their crashed planes even though the planes are made out of plywood. One guy was still in his Quonset hut shaking with a newspaper over his head. Of course the next day, the medics were awfully busy treating cut feet including mine.

Whenever we were able to do so, we were out with the picks to try to cut into the coral rock to make our fox hole a little deeper and of course filling sand bags. When our fox hole was completed, it was approximately three foot by eight foot and about one foot deep cut with picks and surrounded by sand bags.

When we arrived, the Chamarro natives were dressed. The US made them wear clothes. On the island there were four white girls. They were Red Cross volunteers. One of them I saw quite frequently was Merlyn Lampe who served doughnuts and coffee.

By this time I was a smoker, probably about a pack and a half per day. You could only buy Phillip Morris or Old Gold at a nickel per pack. I believe the beer ration was six cans per week.

Our crew flew to twenty bombing mission targets. They were: Iwo Jima, Tokyo, Osaka, Nagoya, Kure, Kobe, Kyushu, Sukumo, Oita, Kawasaki, Sacki, Tokuyama, Yokohama, Tanabe, Hitachi, Hamamatsu, Fukuoka, Sasebo, Kochi and Akaski. The most missions we flew to any one target was seven to Tokyo.

On June 15, 1944, the marines led the assault for control of Saipan followed by the army. More than 30,000 American marines and soldiers were involved in the battle that lasted until July 4th. The cost to capture the island was high; it was one of the bloodiest battles of World War II. There were 3,000 American lives lost compared to 23,000 Japanese.

Then Guam was invaded on July 21, 1944 at a cost of 2,000 Americans and 13,500 Japanese. This was followed by the invasion of Tinian on July 24, 1944 at a cost of 399 Americans and 5,500 Japanese. This made three strategic bases for the B-29's.

I would be remiss if I didn't give credit to the navy for helping to take these islands. My good friend Paul Meyers was on the USS Washington, a battle ship with nine sixteen inch guns. His ship would come within 10,000 to 12,000 feet of enemy guns and would bombard the islands to help soften them up for invading troops. His ship would take evasive action every few moments and could approach the island as close as the deep water would allow.

My position was the top gunner seated in a chair operated like a barber chair. This gave me a 360 degree viewing area from my vantage point. This was located in front of the top rear turret. Depending on the situation, at the flip of a switch, I would give control of one or two of the turrets to the bombadier, the right or left gunner. Approximately, half of the time I fired the remote controlled top forward turret, with four caliber machine guns and the top rear turret with two 50-caliber guns

On December 7, 1944 at four fifteen in the morning Japanese fighter planes came over giving us hell. They came from Iwo Jima. The attack destroyed three B-29s and damaged many more. However our aircraft did shoot down six enemy aircraft. Then on Christmas of 1944 there was a three hour air raid that kept us in our fox holes. The Japanese radio, Tokyo Rose, taunted us about having us in the fox holes on Christmas Day. Then on December 26, there was two more air raids. They really harassed us and we only got two hours of sleep. Of course more followed that.

Island of Kwajalein.

General Emmett O'Donnell
and Lt. Col. Robert Morgan led the first
B-29 mission against Japan on Nov. 24, 1944.

When the Japanese fighters snuck in and strafed our island, our fighters the P-61, the Black Widow and the P-38 Lightning could not fire upon them over Saipan because of the danger to us on the island. They waited a few miles out to sea and shot them down when they came out!

The mess hall usually served Australian mutton, spam, or C rations. We also got dehydrated potatoes and when available, some canned vegetables.

On December 8, 1944, we flew our first mission to Iwo Jima with 10 ton of bombs at 20,000 feet. Right after takeoff there was a huge drop off and an in board engine had to be restarted. We were very lucky we didn't go down into the drink. I was plenty scared but there was no opposition. A mission for a B-29 to Iwo Jima, would not count for a mission for rotation, because they considered it an easier mission or a shakedown mission.

One of the B-29s based in Saipan had to ditch on December 13, 1944, however it did remain a float for 17 hours. Before our next flight which was going to lead to Tokyo, I took the three enlisted gunners with me to the gun mechanic to see that they would be in perfect condition for our flight. On the way back the left gunner Miller said, "You couldn't get him to say what you wanted". That was the first and last check before our missions as it didn't seem necessary.

Then on December 27, 1944 the target was Tokyo for our second mission. Upon reaching landfall, I was so scared I spun around like a top in my barber chair. I was afraid I would miss an incoming fighter. After a short time, I realized I had to calm down and I had to ease the chair around and could spot the fighters quite easily that way. We did drop four, 500 pound general purpose bombs and hit the dock area from 30,000 feet. Six bombs however, landed in the ocean. It seemed like we were over Tokyo for 30 minutes. The head winds could make our ground speed about 60 miles per hour and the tail winds could make us go up to 500 miles per hour.

There was very heavy flak, about 30 fighters. The right gunner shot down Tojo. Tojo approached our B-29 from the rear and the closing speed was quite slow, so our right gunner nailed him pretty easily. So he did bail out, however his chute didn't open, just twisted, and he went, zoom, straight down. Then on the way back, we got lost for a while. Luckily the navigator brought us back safely. Our navigator used a octant to shoot the stars for our position which was an eight sided figure not a sextant which was a six sided figure.

We were given small musical instruments. I got a piccolo and finally learned to play on it, 'Oh sweet and lovely lady be good, be good to me'.

About this time we found out that one of the men was a barber and he set up his chair off to the side of the mail room which was attached to the mess hall and he gave haircuts for 35 cents.

My third mission was a mission to Nagoya, Japan, at an altitude of 30,000 feet. We carried and dropped ten, 500 pound general purpose bombs. There were around 20 fighters. They shot a big hole about one foot above the engineer's head. Luckily we didn't have to bring back a dead engineer. I was worried for the first time on the landing. We flew this mission in Z46, in which we flew five missions.

From the time a person boarded the plane for a mission until it landed safely back at Saipan, it was one hell of a long period of high anxiety.

On January 22, 1945, I received 71 letters from my old APO address. I had a few hours of good ole home news to catch up on.

On January 23, 1945 we flew our fourth mission to Nagoya carrying general purpose and incendiary bombs at an altitude of 26,000 feet. Here they put up 75 to 100 fighters. There were at least five attacks on my position using four plane concentrated attacks. Two B-29's were lost. The left gunner shot down an Irving but he ran out of ammunition in the lower gun turret and burned out the gun barrels. On this mission, there were about 15 to 30 holes in the tail, we had to replace the tail on the plane. What happened was that my guns got hot and they cooked off the fire interrupters do not stop cooked off guns.

Our co-pilot at the time, Lieutenant Taylor took us gunners down by the shore for target practice with our 45 caliber pistols. We threw cans and bottles into the water. We were all having a great time. Then a bunch of soldiers descended upon us with rifles wanting to know if we were trying to start a war. I believe that we would have been in a lot of trouble if the lieutenant wouldn't have been with us.

For the fifth mission I was going on my first night mission to Kobe. It was February 8, 1945. It was my 19th birthday. Our crew was at the Quonset hut, our living quarters on Saipan and we piled into the truck for our ride to the air strip. Upon arrival at the parking place our B-29 was ready to go. We pushed the 17-foot diameter props through to prime the engines and they roared in to life. To start the engines, the four bladed props had to be pushed through two revolutions to be primed. Almost the entire crew did this, two men on a propeller at a time. Because this was a night mission, two gunners were left behind and I sat in the right gunner's position. I watched as we taxied into position for takeoff. The B-29's were so huge and powerful that all else seemed insignificant. The night itself was extremely dark. Weather was very comfortable.

As we jockeyed into line and into position, it took my breath away to see B-29 after B-29 with their intense landing lights piercing the darkness, in what seemed to be an endless line. A sight to behold and never forgotten. Slowly, very slowly we moved forward in the line until we were next for takeoff. When we were in the final position I looked out and saw the chaplain blessing our plane, it was a picture I would remember for a life time and I felt better prepared for the mission ahead. Then our B-29 gathered speed for takeoff down the runway and quickly we were up and on our way.

Z-45 "Mustn Touch" our first mission to Iwo Jima.

Z-52 "20th Century Sweetheart" flew our second mission.

Flew Z-46 "Su Su Baby" on my 3rd mission.

An awesome daylight view of an endless line of B-29's for takeoff.

Major General Curtis LeMay, Commanding General of the
20th Air Force. "No Nonsense-Destroy the Enemy-Win the War."
Ordered low altitude incendiary bombing.

Mount Fujiyama, 12,387 feet.

Lt. Murray Taylor, bottom row, is first person, left to right.

Lt. Murray Taylor visiting me in Mesa, AZ in 1997.

S/Sgt Joe Duban writing home.

Joe with wife, Mae, in 2002.

Master Sergeant Carl Taschinger taking time by
our foxhole.

Carl in 2003.

S/Sgt Ross Mergenthaler looking tough.

Ross with wife, Lana, in 1996.

S/Sgt Edgar Parent doing a little housework.

S/Sgt Edgar Parent visiting me in Meza, AZ in 1999.

Busy in the kitchen are Red Cross girls: (l-r) Betty Sullivan, Marjorie Edward, Dorothy Way, and Merlyn Lampe.

Japanese air raid results on Saipan, December 7, 1944.

Japanese fighter Tony.

Japanese fighter Tojo.

Japanese fighter Zero.

P-61 the "Black Widow" defended Saipan.

P-38 Lightnings defended Saipan.

BETWEEN MISSION ACTIVITIES
SPORTS, POKER, SNAPSHOTS, WATER FIGHTS

The following snapshots are before and after the activities.

Taschinger, Pepi, Parent, and Mergenthaler.

After looking over a plane: (l-r) Ross, John,
Edgar, and Louis.

M/Sgt Carl loaded with ammo.

I am ready for "ground action!"

S/Sgt John Miller washing up.

(l-r) Me, Ross, Carl, Louis and Edgar.

Ross, Louis and Edgar. "Stick out your tongue
and I'll whack you!"

M/Sgt Carl Taschinger and me.

Louis "I'm the boss!"

Ross taking a fake beating from me!

Edgar Parent playing with Japanese dog.

I am taking it easy.

Me and Ross sitting on foxhole.

Attending religious services.

Louis Pepi and Joe Duban lounging.

Picking up mail after chow.

500th Stage and Theater under construction.

Frontal view of a B-29.

Me and Carl in front of a B-29's nose wheels.

The 500th completed theater. Many times we watched
movies sitting in the rain.

Flak damage on Z-46. Over our 35 combat missions, we were riddled with holes many times. Miracle after miracle we were still alive.

Three plane formation of P-51's.

This B-29 did not make it to runway on May 26, 1945
after Tokyo bombing.

Just a few more miles to go back to Saipan. Three of the crew were trapped and drowned.

P-51 escort seen from the right gunner's position.

Interior pilot's compartment in a B-29 showing positions of the
pilot, co-pilot and bombardier.

Cleaning up after the noon meal.

Saipan living quarters.

I am now 86 years old and I can say in my entire life I have never seen or been a part of such awesome scenes. Luckily there was no opposition this mission. If a B-29 crewman was shot down and captured he was subjected to brutal torture from the furious Japanese.

Lieutenant Murray Taylor, who flew as our co-pilot the first four missions, visited me in Mesa, Arizona in 1997. During his visit, he told me he requested a transfer to another crew because our pilot didn't care if he lived or died. At the time I didn't know that the pilot had lost his wife and daughter in a drowning accident.

When we encountered fighters, usually there never seemed to be a lull in the attack. They were fearless fighters and very tenacious. We were lucky on some of the missions they were not Kamikaze suicide fighters.

It seemed if a crew survived the first five missions, the survival chances seemed to increase. Then on February 19, 1945, it was our sixth mission to Tokyo aircraft factory. The bomb load was 6,955 pounds, 13 general purpose bombs, 7,500 rounds of ammunition, 100 B-29s going over the target at 26,000 feet. There were 30 to 45 fighters. I could almost reach out and touch the fighters. A few dived in so close when they turned their belly up the whole sky was blotted out! My guns got so hot they cooked off and I almost shot our tail off. We shot down three fighters. A one foot by one foot hole got shot in our vertical stabilizer.

The plane was riddled with holes from twenty millimeter and caliber thirty ammunition. Left gunner Miller, was wounded in the right hand, pilot Standen was wounded in the left foot. When he took his shoe off, the blood just poured out. I saw one B-29 get rammed and go down in two pieces aflame. Every man of the crew at one time or another came within three feet of being killed by holes in the plane. We came home on three engines, we were told to prepare for crash landing on Saipan. At the time of this mission the bomb bay doors were operated electrically. The landing gear would not come down, we tried everything. The backup system would not work.

The flight engineer Taschinger said he knew of one more method, he climbed out into the bomb bay. At the junction box, he switched the bomb bay circuit to the landing gear circuit which brought the gear down. He also saw two bombs still hanging up which we had to land with, wonderful landing, three man coordination. Our pilot operated the elevators, the co-pilot operated the rudders and the engineer cut engines as soon as we hit the ground. We had to land on a B-24 runway.

Our pilot William, Standen, was awarded the Silver Star for his sixth mission. As of June 1998, there were 102 awards given to the military. The Silver Star was number seven, a very prestigious award.

After this mission Pepi said, "It's a wonder with all these missions that we are still alive, we have been awfully lucky" Miller says, "somebody up there must be watching over us." Then Parent said, "I know, there are angels on our shoulders".

On February 27, 1945, another one of our planes had to ditch in the ocean. It failed to make it back from Saipan by just a few miles. Three of the crew were trapped and drown.

My seventh mission was a night mission. We carried 10 - 500 pound general purpose bombs and all guns were loaded with 200 rounds. We had to bomb a target of opportunity, the naval base of Sukumo at 27,000 feet. We gave a report at Guam and then headed back to Saipan.

Sometimes Japanese fighters would come out from Iwo Jima to engage B-29's on their way to Japan. When we were out of the danger zone, I would sit on the floor until we approached the danger zone of Japan. Then Captain Standen always alerted us saying, "Landfall ahead". There was no need for me to alert my gunners, I knew they were ready and watchful like me covering their positions.

When we met up with enemy fighters, the intercom came alive with the gunners chatter of incoming fighters from all directions. It all happened very quickly as closing speed was in split seconds.

The fighters would come 3 or 4 at a time. We would fire at the first one and then the ones that followed. The action was happening at hair-trigger speed so it was impossible to know what happened to any of our targets.

The sunsets over the ocean, red and orange were just beautiful. It was hard to believe that we were headed for a target with probable fighters and anti-aircraft fire.

On March 13, 1945. I flew my eighth mission, which was a night mission over Osaka, Japan, the second largest city of 3.5 million. We burned the hell out of it with 14,200 pounds of incendiary bombs. I was really scared and had a rosary in my hand the whole time. The altitude over the target was 6,800 feet. No guns except the tail guns. I rode the left blister. Miller and Pepi stayed behind. There were tracers, fire, searchlights, smoke.

Suddenly over the target everything went completely black. This was the first time I had flown through smoke. I felt like I was being tossed around like a feather in a wind storm. Later I learned it was the thermal heat in the smoke. I was going to bail out since nobody answered my repeated questions of, "What happened, what happened?" I thought everyone was dead and we were about to crash. The pilot battling the controls stopped me just in time saying, "We are in the smoke!"

It is really incredible that a B-29 weighing seventy-five tons when loaded with bombs, could be flipped over onto its back from the thermal heat and the smoke, it did happen, but not to us!

One day we needed a fifth poker player and we introduced Marion Stevens from another crew to the game teaching him the rules. The second hand we played was a good sized pot and Miller started dragging in the pot with two big pairs. Marion says, "Gee, as all as I had was three eights!"

On March 16, 1945 the crew went on a mission except Miller and I who stayed at home, they burned the hell out of Kobe. They had taken tail guns only.

Flew Z-54 "Helles Belles" on our 7th mission. We flew 14 missions on this B-29. The most missions on any one B-29.

My CFC top gunner's position was in the small bubble just in
front of the rear turret.

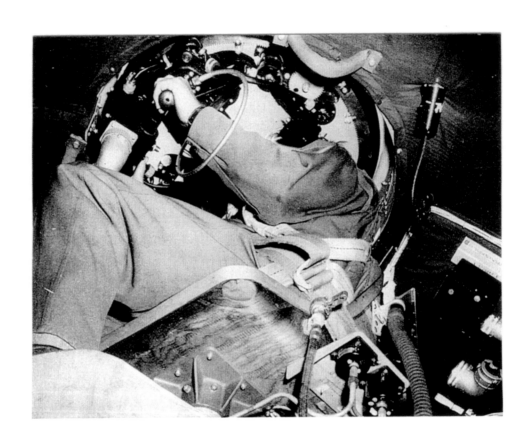

Interior picture of a Central Fire Control top gunner's position.

A Central Fire Control top gunner's post has a 360 degree viewing area.

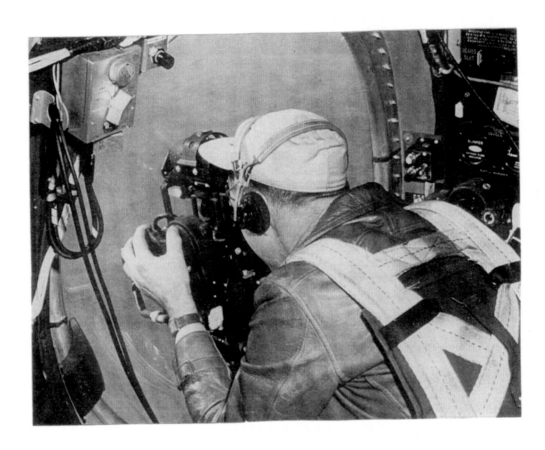

Right side gunner using remote gun sight.

This B-29 remained afloat 17 hours after ditching on
December 13, 1944.

On this B-29's 12th mission it burned after landing on Iwo Jima with battle damage in 1945.

Saipan Tinian Channel.

"Irish Lassie" crew survived on January 27, 1945.

A ditched plane and notice off to the right the crew in life rafts.

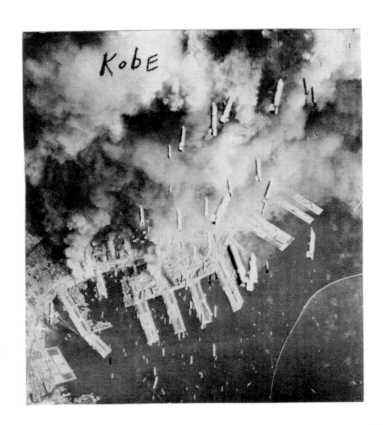

Incendiary bombs starting large fires on June 5, 1945, target Kobe.

Results of bombing Kure.

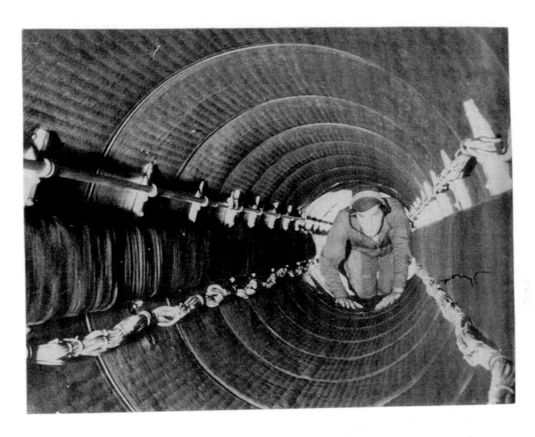

This shows the forty foot tunnel connecting the pilot's
and gunner's compartments.

The guys were gathered around one of the bunks. I went over and saw an airman sound asleep with his eyes wide open, they were glazed over. I never saw anything like that before, just amazing.

On March 24th it was my ninth mission to the Nagoya aircraft factory. We carried 31-540 pound bombs. Two were incendiaries. We had to salvo bombs through the bomb bay doors. They ripped the door right in half. To this day I do not know why, but our crew had to bomb through the bomb bay doors, which means we had to dump the bombs in the ocean. Later in the mission we lost the number three engine had to feather it and limp home on three engines again. They did catch us in the searchlights and luckily they did not hit us. We had tail guns only and this mission was carried on at an altitude of 6,500 feet.

Each mission we went on we were supplied with a huge bag of orange marmalade sandwiches.

My tenth mission on March 27th was a mission to Oita, we carried 14 – 500 pound general purpose bombs. We did hit the target from an altitude of 15,000 feet. We carried 200 rounds per gun. It was a day mission, however they did hit us with flak in the bomb bay doors, but the damage was minimal so it was of no concern.

I said to Miller, "How many people do you think we kill and injure when we drop our bombs? Two, three thousand you think? It must really be hell down there!" Miller said, "Don't think about it, keep it out of your mind, we just have to do our job."

April 4, 1945, was my 11th mission. We hit the Tokyo aircraft factory with 36 - 500 pound general purpose delayed action bombs and four photoflash bombs. We were in the search lights quite a while. We were at an altitude of 6,000 feet. This was a night mission. We did have to salvo 11 bombs, however. The only thing we had for defense was the tail guns.

The side gunner blisters on rare occasions have been known to blow out completely. So there was one crewman, a side gunner from another crew that thought he would take no chances. He made himself a 16 to 20 foot long safety belt, so if anything would ever happen to him and he went out, they could get him. Actually his blister did blow out and they were able to pull him back into safety.

One side gunner on another crew got sucked out of the plane and was lost when his blister blew out. It happened just after leaving the target.

My 12th mission was a night mission to the Tokyo area of Kawasaki; we carried 34 – 500 pound general purpose bombs and two flare bombs. We hit them at an altitude of 6,000 feet. Kawasaki was a secondary target. There was no fighter opposition on this target.

On April 7, 1945 we were awarded the Distinguished Flying Cross for flying our 13th mission, a day mission, at an altitude of 15,000 feet to the Tokyo area, to bomb the Makashino aircraft plant. We had five 2,000 pound general purpose bombs. We had the P51s out of Iwo Jima for fighter protection. The Japanese put up about 200 fighters, we got over 45 fighter attacks on our plane. We had 7,500 rounds of ammunition. Two or three attempts were made to ram us, and then a Jap fighter came at us at 12:00 position, straight on. I thought my life was over! Our pilot at the last second took evasive action and pulled the plane up so sharply that the B-29 just shook. Our tail gunner said that the plane missed our tail guns by about six inches.

There were caliber 30 holes in our tail and on the number four engine. A 20 millimeter hole in the right wing. Our lower rear turret and our lower forward turret were destroyed by anti-aircraft fire. They even dropped phosphorus bombs in an attempt at air to air bombing. Our left gunner, bombadier, and I claimed probable or kills. I got credit for a kill. We had to feather number four engine after leaving landfall and were unable to make it to Saipan. We had to land at Iwo Jima. We slept that night in our plane and went from Iwo Jima to Saipan on a C-46 the next day.

For mission number 13, by direction of the president under the provisions of the Act of Congress approved July 2, 1926 announcement is made of the award of the Distinguished Flying Cross. For extraordinary achievement while participating in an aerial flight over Japan on April 7, 1945 each individual was a member of a B-29 crew which participated in an unprecedented medium altitude delayed attack on the Makashino aircraft plant in Tokyo, Japan.

The citation read: Enemy opposition was extraordinarily effective and the aircraft suffered severe battle damage from intense enemy aircraft fire throughout the bomb run. The aircraft was rendered incapable of maximum protective fire because of the destruction of its lower turrets by enemy anti-aircraft fire. At lands' end a deliberate collision by enemy aircraft was avoided by a violent climb. The enemy pressed unrelenting fire attacks until the point thirty miles out to sea was reached. Because of the damage of instrumental aids, the aircraft made its three engine flight back to its home base under the most unfavorable navigational conditions and was under constant danger of a forced landing hundreds of miles out to sea in enemy waters. The mental stability under fire, the courage and high professional skills displayed by these individuals resulted in a most efficient and highest degree of cooperation in the emergencies encountered in this mission and reflect great credit on themselves and the army air forces.

On night missions, we usually got caught in the searchlights, which reached well over 20,000 feet. I felt like I was a bull's-eye. You could actually read a newspaper and many times their anti-aircraft fire was very accurate.

My 14th mission on April 13 , 1945, was a night mission to Tokyo. We were in the searchlights for five to seven minutes. Something we really didn't like. We bombed by radar and burned out over ten square miles of Tokyo causing more damage than the atomic bomb. On night missions, to fool the radar, we would throw out three rolls of tin foil several times.

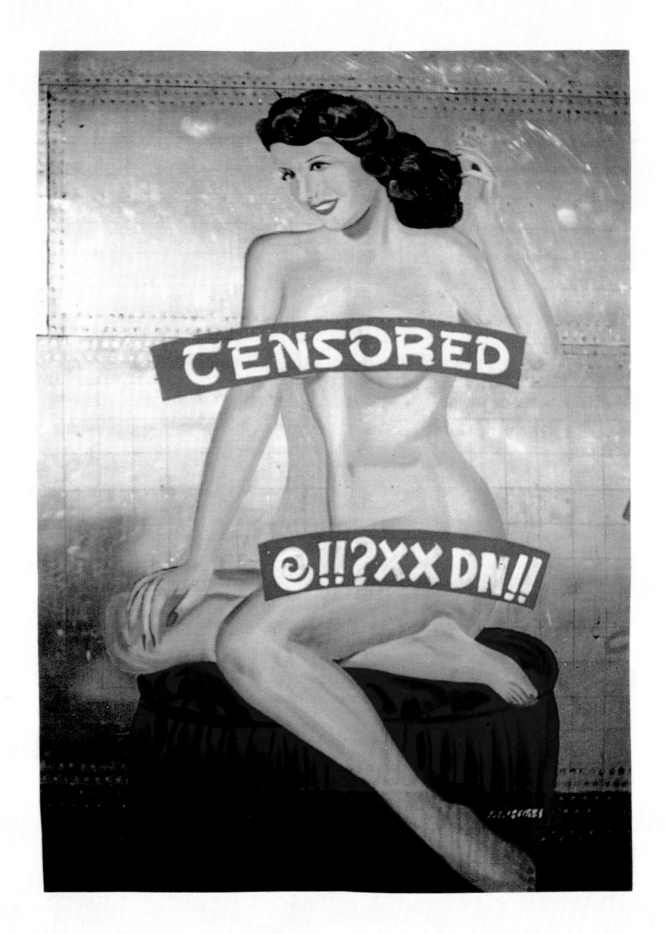

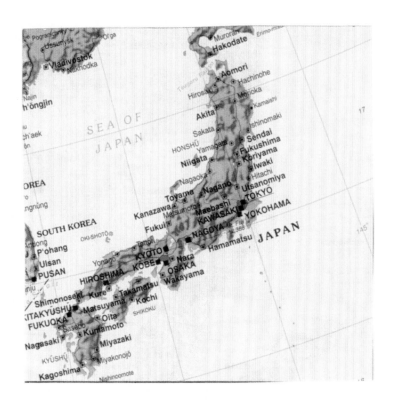

Map of Japan.

The incendiary bomb clusters scattered after the metal bands binding them together break at a predetermined altitude above the ground. When they hit the ground, they light up like matches and cover an area of 2,500 feet long and 500 feet wide. There were as many as 800 B-29s scheduled to fly on a single mission.

On April 30, 1945 we were scheduled to fly a mission to Truk. Well, what do you know, we get a milk run, an easy mission to Truk. This would not be counted as a mission for rotation. We navigated P-47 Thunderbolts to strafe. We decided to strafe a radar shack on a small island with our own guns while waiting for the P-47s. After we quit strafing, our guns were not stowed properly, cooked off and knocked out our number three engine. It lost all the oil in the engine and the prop spun off.

When this happens, it goes left and cuts a fuseluge in half or goes right and knocks out the number four engine. In either case you would be lost at sea. I was doing a lot of praying. Somebody must have been watching over us, because it came off, flew forward about a foot, then up and back completely missing our plane. I actually believed I witnessed a miracle even though it seems we already had more than our share. I made a report after each mission about the approximate number of ammunition used. This time the pilot told me not to make out an ammunition report.

However, incredibly against all odds there actually were B-29's that lost two engines on the same side that did make it back from Japan. The first was Lt. Chico Carrico. This remarkable feat was repeated by Capt. James Pearson and by Capt. Feathers

The protective armor and the 20 millimeter gun in the tail was removed in early March so more bombs could be carried. A tail gunner from another crew stuck a broom out of the tail so he could fool the Japanese into thinking he still had a twenty millimeter gun. Two side gunners were along to watch the engines.

Often times a big element of keeping us alive is overlooked, certainly not intentionally. The ground crew, the mechanics, the armament personnel, and the body work men kept us in the air! A tremendous amount of credit belongs to them. We thank you! Thank you!

April 17th my 15th mission was a mission to Kyushu airfield. We carried 32 - 260 pound fragmentation bombs at an altitude of 15,000 feet. We had 500 rounds per gun. This was a day mission, but there was no opposition. We hit the primary target visually.

There were three crews in our barracks. All noncoms approximately 20 men. The other two crews would occasionally get a bottle of whiskey from their officers on their crew. We never did, so finally a couple of our guys went over and asked for one. Then all three crews had a wild party. Jonesy from another crew threw an empty beer can and hit our left gunner Miller in the forehead. Miller grabbed for his 45 pistol and Jonesy shot out the door into the black night, with Miller after him. Our barracks was quiet as a mouse, we were just listening for a shot.

About an hour later, Miller came back and sat on his bunk and we gathered around him and he quickly ejected a shell from his 45, he intended to kill Jonesy. He set the 45 beside him and one of our guys grabbed it. I give him credit, I wouldn't have tried it. Pretty soon our pilot came in and sat beside Miller and said that Jonesy had come over to his Quonset "What's this I hear about you wanting to shoot him?" Miller said, "I'm OK now" Pilot Standen said, "Well he isn't coming back, he is staying with us for the night".

Generally speaking, most of our fighter opposition declined during our tour of duty, shortly after those fire blitz raids began in March of 1945. However it never declined much over Tokyo or over naval base Kure. They were the most heavily defended and their fighters flew right through the flak bursts.

On April 20th, Miller and Standen were awarded the Purple Heart. On April 22nd, I was credited with a destroyed Tony from the April 7th mission, Miller a damage and Trotter a damage. Therefore the crews standing was Miller – a kill and damage, Pepi – a kill and damage, and Trotter – a kill and damage, and me a kill.

After my last mission I asked who will take my bet, I say we get orange marmalade sandwiches for our next mission, any takers?? Ross said, "Nothing like betting on a sure thing!"

My 16th mission was a mission to the Saki naval air base on April 25th. We carried 17 - 500 pound general purpose bombs. It was a daylight mission. We were supposed to have bombed at 13,000 feet, but the weather didn't permit, so we had to bomb at 23,000 feet and we bombed by radar. No enemy opposition.

Sometimes we would get a ride in the back of a truck, standing room only, to go to one of the beaches to dive for shells. On one occasion, the driver slammed on his brakes at about 50 miles per hour and my head got slammed into the cab. My head and my ears really hurt for quite a while, but later on seemed to be OK. The shells that we got, we put under the barracks for the ants to eat out so they kept their shine. Then necklaces and earrings were made out of them.

We did have some real fun. We had a lot of water fights and one night when we were in the bunks someone heard a mouse scampering along and yelled, "Air raid!" and dumped lighter fluid on the wood floor and lit it. Everyone got out their flashlights sweeping the hut like search lights. Then everyone was slamming their shoes trying to get the mouse.

May 4, 1945 was our 17th mission, a day mission to Kure aircraft factory. We flew at 23,000 feet. There was severe flak damage including a number two engine getting hit and a cracked right blister. There were also holes in the right wing and a gash in the aileron and the radio compass got hit. The flak was extremely dangerous and was really pretty, it was all different colors. Upon return, due to fuel being dangerously low, we were unable to fly a landing pattern. Luckily we hit the runway when the engines cut out barely making it back. We even had to be towed to our parking place.

On April 30, 1945, we navigated 20-P47 Thunderbolts to
by-passed Island Truk to strafe them.

Flew Z-47 "Adam's Eve" on our 15th mission.

My 16th mission was on Z-51 "Tail Wind". We flew 3
missions on this plane.

Flew Z-50 "Fancy Detail" on our 17th mission bombing Kure.

The flight time for each mission was 13 to 16 hours depending on a head or tail wind. By the time all my missions were completed, I had flown over the ocean more than 120,000 miles.

On the way back from Kure, a P-51 fighter, one of our guardian angels, followed us to Iwo Jima for its landing. He needed us for navigational purposes. We would show him with our fingers 100, 80, 60 miles to go to Iwo Jima. When Iwo Jima was in sight, he put on an air show which was incredible to show his thanks and happiness for getting back alive. He made loops and turns and spins. One hell of a show!

Usually someone would clown around in the barracks. Our tail gunner, Eddie Parent held his fingers to his eyes making them slanty and said, " Me Tojo shoot down all dogs on B-29 planes" right gunner Louie Pepi says, "We are gunna make all Japanese fighters happy to join their honorable ancestors".

May 9, 1945 was my 18th mission, a daylight mission to the Tokuyama open oil and gasoline storage tanks and refineries. We hit the target causing black columns of smoke up to 15,000 feet and huge fires were started. The bombing altitude was 19,000 feet. We dropped 20 - 500 pound general purpose bombs on the target. Two of them hung up in the racks. There were 400 B-29s that participated in this mission. The flak over the target was inaccurate. There were 14 Jap war ships throwing up meager but accurate flak. After each mission, each man got a shot of whiskey. I never liked it, so I gave mine to left gunner Miller.

On May 14th we were scheduled to go on a mission at Nagoya. There were 600 B-29s scheduled. However we had to abort the mission. We dropped our incendiaries ten miles out, 425 pounds, because the landing gear would not come up.

We clowned around with first sergeant stripes belonging to flight engineer Carl Taschinger giving orders and threatening each other with a stick.

On May 16th, my 19th mission was to Nagoya. We had 40 - 465 pound incendiary clusters. Large fires were started. The search lights did not pick us up. We of course threw out our rope of tin foil. The left gunner was in the hospital due to an infected leg, so he wasn't along. The altitude we flew at was 9,100 feet and we had to bomb by radar.

Once between missions, we washed the wings with gasoline to get a bit more speed. I thought about the home folks rationing their gas. It sure took a lot of gas to wash those wings.

My 20th mission was a night mission to Tokyo. We carried 40 – 425 pound incendiary bombs. We bombed by radar at 11,200 feet. Large fires were started. Huge searchlights pierced the sky looking to lock onto a B-29. They managed to lock onto us for about thirty seconds. The flak that they threw up was moderate and accurate, you could really hear it. We got hit by the rear door. This mission was supposed to have killed 1 million people if it was successful. Upon landing, our flaps wouldn't come down but 15 degrees. I was scared as usual, like I was on all missions. We also had an oil leak on the number two engine.

Right gunner Pepi and I were assigned to drive one of the two jeeps which were to patrol the air strip and guard against enemy paratroopers. Neither of us knew how to drive. We argued who would try to drive, I won. The officer of the day drove us up to the air strip and I was praying they would let the jeep running because I didn't know how to start it. We heard they raced each other, so as I drove away, here comes a jeep behind me, so I really stepped on the gas. It was the officer of the day, he said, "Here you forgot your rain coat!"

We also heard that on the other side of the island there was a place we could go to get coffee. It was pitch dark and we decided to go see if we could find it. We got about half way and the lights went out on the jeep. Pepi held his flash light and we tried to keep going. Then someone yelled, "Halt!" and he steered us right and we got back onto the air strip. There was of course still Japs loose on the island. We were lucky they didn't kill us and lucky we didn't get caught and charged with deserting our post. We were young and foolish.

May 29, 1945 was my 21st mission to Yokohama. One of my 50-caliber guns would not test fire, but we couldn't do anything about it and had to fly to the target anyway. Col. Dougherty was in the lead ship and we were number three in the third element of the lead squadron. We bombed visually from 18,100 feet with 148 – 70 pound incendiary bombs. Large fires were started.

We encountered moderate to accurate flak which I could hear exploding. The P-51s escorted us. I spotted two enemy fighters. One started an attack from 11:00 position high and got scared away by our top six guns. As of this date, there were over 1,000 men lost out of the wings so far.

B-29s bombed Osaka, Tokyo, Nagoya, Kure and several less known cities by day and night. On just one night in March of 1945 B-29s fire bombing on Tokyo destroyed 16 square miles, leaving one million homeless and 150,000 dead, missing or injured.

Our opposition ran as high at 200 aircraft. Some B-29s were hit by suicide pilots and went down. From April 1944 to August 1945, there were 414 B-29s with their 11-man crews in combat and 114 B-29s lost in non-combat. In a single day there were six cities wiped out. By August 1945, Tokyo and 64 other Jap cities were destroyed.

We flew our missions on 11 different planes. Fourteen of those missions were flown on the same plane Z-54. The same plane usually was assigned to different flight crews. We flew Z-45 on our first mission. It was lost with another crew on January 12, 1945. We had flown four missions on Z-46 when another crew flew it and it was lost at sea on March 7, 1945. Another plane we flew, Z-47 also was lost with its crew on April 7, 1945.

Other reasons we flew different planes was because they were shot down, crashed on takeoff or landing, or the ground crew had to repair and service those that had extensive combat damage, mechanical problems or needed engine changes.

Bombing of Yokohama on May 29, 1945, my 21st mission.
Col. Dougherty was in the lead B-29.

Colonel John E. Dougherty. 500th Bombardment Group
Commander. "Gallantry above and beyond the call of duty."

Z-58, "Sweet Eloise" heading for target Japan.

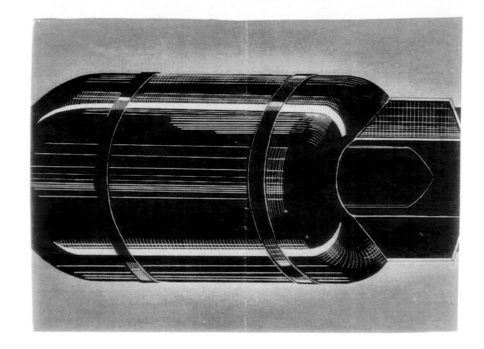

SHEET NO. 1 (Back of the bomb)

No. 1 Priority = Maintain your health

No. 2 Priority = Medicine

- The USA will continue to bomb until the Japanese military regime surrenders.
- Everybody knows that the USA has the power to continue bombing until Japan is in shambles.
- The Japanese military regime only continues the war because they are afraid of being punished
- You are all probably puzzled by the war.
- All the people are being punished for the egos of a few.
- You must ask your leaders to stop this desperate war.
- This is the only way to avoid more bombing.

Bomb leaflet and interpretation.

工業地帯居住者へ！

やがて我が空爆は益々猛烈になる爲めに
我軍は工業地帯居住者の君達に立ち退き
を警告します、我々は空襲にて君達市民
に怪我をさせたり殺したくありません、
君達が工業地帯を立退いて始めて我軍は
君達の尊い命を助ける事が出来るのです
工場や軍需工場は軍事的目標なのです、
軍隊に其所を守らせ給へ！

No. 2036

SHEET NO. 2

To Plant Area Residents !

- We give warning to plant *(factory)* area residents that you should take refuge because our bombing grows increasingly worse and worse.
- We do not want to hurt the general population with our bombing.
- We can help you if you take refuge away from the plant areas.
- The plants or munitions plants are the target of our millitary.
- You should make your millitary protect the plants ! *(note: I'm not sure why they added this sentence)*

Endless B-29's propaganda leaflet with interpretation.

日本國民
諸氏
アメリカ合衆
國大統領
ハリー・エス
ツルーマン
より一書を
呈す

十千久獨逸は壊滅せり　日本國民諸氏も我米國陸海空軍の絶大なる攻撃力を認識せんならむ

貴國為政者並に軍部が戦争を継続する限り我が攻撃は愈々その破壊及び行動を擴大強化し日本の作戦を支持する軍需生産

着送その他人的資源に至る迄徹底的に壊滅せずんば熄まず　戦争の持久は日本國民の艱苦を徒らに増大するのみ而も國民の得る處は絶無なり　我が攻撃は日本軍部が無條件降伏に屈し武器を棄てる迄は断じて中止せず　軍部の無條件降伏の一般國民に及ぼす影響如何　一言にて盡くせばそは戦争の終焉を意味す　日本を現在の如き破滅の淵に誘引せる軍部の権力を消滅せしめ前線に悪戦苦闘中なる陸海将兵の愛する家族農村或は職場への迅速なる復帰を可能ならしめ且又儚なき戦勝を夢見て現在の艱難苦痛を永続するを止むるを意味す

蓋し無條件降伏は日本國民の抹殺乃至奴隷化を意味するものに作らざる事を断言して憚らず

NO. 2088

SHEET NO. 4 (Harry Truman message)

- The military regime will not end the war until they have completely destroyed all of your resources.
- The continuation of this war increases the pain in your country and does not gain you anything.
- Our attacks cannot be stopped until the military regime accepts an unconditional surrender.
- How big of an impact will an unconditional surrender have? In other words, it means ending the war.
- Stopping the war means that the power of the military that ruins your country will be ended.
- Stopping the war means that the members of the military, navy and air force may return home to their families, villages and offices.
- It means that the entire empty dream of victory and the continuation of the pain can end.
- Therefore, I do not hesitate to declare that an unconditional surrender will not thoroughly enslave your nation.

Propaganda leaflet-President Harry Truman, with interpretations.

June 1, 1945 was my 22nd combat mission going to Osaka. It was one of our day missions from Saipan. We carried 29 - 420 pound incendiary bombs. On this mission, we were fortunate to have P-51s escorting us from their base in Iwo Jma. On high altitude day missions, sometimes we would leave a vapor trail, which was a huge disappointment for us because it gave a much better target for their anti-aircraft guns.

One late morning there were four poker players ready to play, but they didn't have a fifth player. Miller said, "Wake up Heiberger, he will play." Parent said, "Cripes, are you crazy, he always wins!" The desire to play won over logic and they woke me up.

My 23rd mission, on June 5, 1945, was a day mission to Kobe. We bombed visually with 178 – 70 pound incendiary bombs. The smoke rose to 20,000 feet. I had two attacks from 12:00 and 2:30 positions. The bombadier and I damaged a fighter. A hole got shot in our tail turret. We had bad weather and flew through sleet and hail.

This was the last mission to Kobe. After this bombing the target wasn't worth revisiting. There were many other times we flew through bad weather also. On this mission 450 superforts dropped 3000 tons of incendiary bombs. A Japanese news agency reported 56 Superforts were shot down and 144 heavily damaged

On June 7, 1945 my 24th mission, we flew through sleet and hail on a day mission to Osaka. Our altitude was 20,000 feet. We bombed by radar with incendiary bombs with complete cloud coverage and it was very meager flak. We had to land on Iwo Jima short of gas and ripped right tire. The next morning the Japs came out of their caves on a banzai attack but we had already left.

Due to the valiant effort of our marines and army and at an alarming cost, Iwo Jima was secured. By war's end 2,400 B-29 bombers carrying 27,000 crew members had made emergency landing on Iwo Jima. I salute the marines and army for having made it possible for us to land there.

Prisoners were starved, beaten and denied medical attention. The Japanese took a B-29 navigator's clothes away on a very cold day and then caged him like a wild circus animal with his hands tied to the front bars because he could hardly stand. Then they paraded him through the streets. His body was covered with bloody sores from bedbugs, lice and flees. By this time he thought he had lost 90 pounds, but during this ordeal, in his words, he was trying to act like an Air Force guy.

As I have mentioned, going on missions was always scary. You wondered what lies ahead, adverse weather, ditching in the ocean, fighters, flak, engine trouble, being captured by the Japanese. Since we carried a 45 pistol, some wondered what they would do. You pretty much kept that thought out of your mind and climbed aboard.

June 10, 1945, my 25th mission we carried seven, 2,000 pound general purpose bombs. It was a day mission and there was meager to moderate accurate flack, however there was no fighter attack. The altitude was 20,000 feet. The primary visual target was 357 which was Tokyo and Osaka and there was a lot of cloud cover. So, we bombed Hitachi visually with good results. I had heard the saying the flak was so thick you could walk on it. There were some missions when I was looking ahead, I could see flack so thick right at our altitude I thought there was no way we could fly through it and still be alive. We of course could not take any evasive action on a bomb run.

June 15, 1945 was the 26th day mission to Osaka. We bombed by radar. Our right gunner and pilot were sick. Lieutenant Col. Parsons flew pilot and Vangandt flew right gunner. We had 33 - 465 pound incendiaries. We flew in the soup over an hour wing tip to wing tip in a two plane formation. It looked to me that the wing tips were only a few feet apart and that they would collide as they hovered up and down. It was a tremendous relief to me when this mission was completed.

Our crew flew 30 missions over the homeland of Japan without fighter escort. There was none the first 12 missions, none on night missions, and none when there was unfavorable weather over the target.

The P-51 Mustang escorts were assigned to the 7th fighter group on Iwo Jima. On one occasion they lost thirty P-51s going through a storm from Iwo Jima to Japan. Only three pilots survived.

A general was to fly in and they had us all up on the tarmac standing at attention in Class-A uniform in the hot sun. Several guys passed out, that was very understandable since normally we had just a pair of shorts on and no marching detail or KP.

On June 4th I was promoted to staff sergeant and on June 16th I was awarded the Air Medal. You would first get the Air Medal for the first seven combat missions that you had and then every seven combat missions after that you were awarded the Bronze Oak Leaf Cluster.

Now the Air Medal is awarded by the direction of the president, under the provisions of the executive order. It reads for meritorious achievement while participating in aerial flights as combat crew members in successful combat missions in bases in the Marianas Islands against the Japanese empire. These missions were flown under rapidly changing and often times adverse weather conditions. The flights were subjected to intense enemy anti-aircraft fire and fighter opposition. There were constantly present difficult navigational problems, dangerous mechanical failure and consequential ditching many miles out to sea. Under a prolonged period of physical and mental strain and undaunted by the many hazards faced regularly and continuously, each crew member displayed much courage and skill in the performance of his duty as to reflect great credit on himself and the army air forces.

Fires burning Osaka on June 1, 1945, my 22nd mission. P-51's, those guardian angels escorted us.

Iwo Jima flag raising.

On Z-53 "Ancient Mariner" we flew 5 missions in June 1945 encountering severe storms and flak. Our wings damaged by anti-aircraft flak.

Our pilot sick so our pilot was Lt. Col. Freeman A. Parsons on
26th mission to Osaka.

Between missions we played a lot of basketball and baseball. After a game, Carl Taschinger, our flight engineer, was always back to the barracks first. He just sat on his bunk and slid his feet into his wooden shower shoes and rushed out the door. One day we nailed the shower shoes to the floor and he almost did a cartwheel.

I received a letter from my brother, who was serving in a tank corps in Germany, he wrote saying, "It is a million dollars' worth of experience, but I wouldn't give you a nickel for it". I told one of the fellows and he said, "I will tell you what, I can think of a million places I would rather be".

On June 17, 1945 I flew my 27th mission, a night mission at 8,700 feet. The target was Hamamatsu. We carried 184 – 70 pound incendiaries. Our pilot was still sick. The pilot was Captain Black. We bombed by radar due to complete cloud coverage. It was a short mission, just a little over 12 hours. There wasn't any flak, or fighters or search lights.

Bob Hope entertained us at our ocean side theater. With him were Jerry Cologna, Vera Vague and Frances Langford. The entertainment was excellent and it was a very nice "time out" from the war, very relaxing!

After a mission, I could really sleep, and I mean sleep soundly and long. The poker players would wake me up to play poker. I won all the time until the last month when it looked to me like I would make it back home alive. I lost my months' pay plus $50 borrowed from the right gunner.

On June 19, 1945 I flew my 28th mission, a night mission to Fukuoka. We carried 40 - 425 incendiary bombs. We bombed by radar. The city was really burning when we reached there. The altitude was 9,100 feet, we encountered major and inaccurate flak. The search lights didn't pick us up. We flew through another one of those storms on the way back.

Ross said it's hard to believe we made it back again. I said "We still must have those angels on our shoulders."

Miller, Pepi and I were assigned one night to guard a B-29. We each had a candy bar, when we finished eating it we would just toss the wrapper away. It was a very nice quiet night, and we heard a paper rustling so we shined our flash lights on the paper wrappers and a mouse scampered away. We thought we would try to catch it.

We turned a bucket upside down and had a piece of wood to hold the side of the bucket up with a long cord attached to it and placed the candy wrapper under the bucket. When we would hear the wrapper rustle, we would pull the cord. The mouse kept coming back. On about the third time we caught it, and slipped a piece of ply wood underneath the bucket, turned it upright and looked in to see the mouse. It shot right up out of that bucket! We caught it again and this time put a rock on top of the ply wood and left it for the ground crew. Sure wish I could have seen the expression on their faces when that mouse shot out of there!

My 29th mission was a day mission to Kure. We visually bombed the target and missed the target, dammit! The altitude was 18,000 feet; we encountered intense black and white flak. We could actually see shrapnel flying. We got hit in the right wing and left wing.

My 30th mission was a day mission to Osaka. We carried seven, 2,000 general purpose bombs. We bombed by radar through full cloud coverage. We didn't know if we hit the target. We were at 23,000 feet and each B-29 was bombing individually.

I commented, you would think we are on the home stretch. Thousands and thousands of Japanese have died along with their cities. It is a lop-sided war, it looks like they will never surrender and will be totally annihilated.

Then on June 28th, my 31st mission, our crew was on a night mission to Sasebo, Japan's most western city. We bombed by radar with 29 – 500 pound incendiaries at an altitude of 10,500 feet. We did have to feather the number two engine an hour and half from the base. There was meager light anti-air craft fire but it was very accurate.

This is the fifth time we had to fly back on three engines, losing one to enemy fire or engine failure. Each time it was a long way back to Saipan over miles and miles of ocean. I sweated and prayed that the other three engines would get us back.

On July 1, 1945 my 32nd mission, we had a night mission to Kyushu. We bombed by radar again with full cloud coverage, with 33 – 500 pound incendiaries at 11,300 feet. There was meager light inaccurate anti-aircraft fire. We had one photo flash bomb.

When we were pressurized at high altitudes, we would crawl through the 40 foot tunnel as fast as we could with orange marmalade sandwiches, which the kitchen always made up for us for every mission. If something happened we would be depressurized when you were in that tunnel you would be shot out of the tunnel like a cannon ball.

Once when I delivered the marmalade to the pilot's compartment pilot Standen said, "We are now on automatic pilot, see if you can turn the flight control". I braced my feet and with every bit of strength I had, I tried turning it. I pulled and pulled and gave it everything I got, but it wouldn't budge. I kept trying. Standen finally said, "That's enough" I think he realized how foolish he was and when I gave it some thought, I thought it was pretty foolish too. I might have spun that B-29 into a roll that it might not have come out of and it could have crashed.

My 33rd mission was a night mission to Kochi on July 3, 1945. I was sitting in the right gunner's seat. We were speeding down the runway to take off. Bushels of spark flew back from the number three engine. I said, "Number three engine on fire sir!" the pilot asked me if we could take off, I told him to go ahead! If I had been wrong, we would have crashed into the ocean with ten tons of bombs on board!

Flew Z-58 "Sweet Eloise" on our 27th mission.

Crew in flight suits.

It was determined later that luckily it was only excess oil burning off. We bombed by radar through full cloud coverage at 11,300 feet. We carried 40 – 500 pound incendiary bombs. The smoke rose to 18,000 feet. There was no flak, no search lights, no enemy fighters. We flew through the smoke over the target, it tore up floors and tail, radar rooms, and central fire control compartments.

Occasionally propaganda leaflets were dropped. There was a picture of a bomb, another with endless B-29s and a third with President Truman's picture, all of them had messages in Japanese.

Then on July 6, 1945 my 34th mission, was a night mission to Akaski. We bombed by radar with 40 – 500 pound incendiaries at an altitude of 7,000 feet. There was no trouble, we flew through the soup.

When a crew has completed 35 combat missions over the homeland of Japan, whether a crew member missed a mission because of sickness or any other circumstance, he also gets credit for that mission.

At the writing of this story, Ross Mergenthaler and I are the only crew survivors. We still correspond with each other. Our crew was very close to one another, and we all exchanged Christmas cards.

By the end of my tour, 35 combat missions, I was credited with two destroyed and one damage. I had been awarded the Marskman Medal for the forty five pistol, the Expert Medal for the sub machine gun, and carbine, the Good Conduct Medal, the Air Medal with Four Bronze Oak Leaf Clusters, the Distinguished Flying Cross, the World War II victory medal, the Asiatic Pacific Theater Medal with three bronze battle stars and the Presidential Unit Citation.

Several days before leaving Saipan, our pilot Standen, said he was promoting me to tech sergeant but the orders never arrived before I left the island.

The plane, Enola Gay, named after the captain Paul Tibbet's, mother, dropped the first 9,500 pound atomic bomb, nick named "Little Boy" on August 6, 1945 on the city of Hiroshima, Japan, leaving 78,000 dead, and 51,000 injured, virtually destroying the entire city. The mushroom cloud from the blast rose past twenty thousand feet.

Three days later a second 11,000 pound atomic bomb nicknamed "Fat Man", was dropped on Nagasaki by the Bockscar, commanded by Major Chuck Sweeney, in a flash, 35,000 died, thousands were injured and the city lay in ruins. This brought the empire of Japan to its knees and the result was a quick closure to the war with Japan. At the time of the first atomic bomb dropped, I was already on my way to the states as my tour of duty, 35 combat missions over the homeland of Japan, was completed.

 I must give credit and say that we had a great crew. Every man and I mean everyman, saved, or helped to save the entire crew in some way. For us gunners, everything was really busy with fighters swarming around us, like angry bees. So it was really hard to say how many we shot down when you needed two witnesses.

Finally it was time to go home, and after flying to Saipan and flying all those missions, I got stuck on a slow boat home. The AK-114 which I called the USS All-Bran because that is all we got to eat. It took us nine days to get home. At one point on the way back, they put up a weather balloon. It must have been about six to eight feet across and used it for gunnery practice. They started firing when it had barely left the boat and the thing flew out of sight without getting hit. I did enjoy watching the flying fish for hours at a time. Something I had seen in the funny papers and didn't really know they existed.

Then on August 8, 1945 we arrived at Seattle, Washington. We were there for the evening meal. We were used to, what I would call, poor food and now all this good rich food was there to eat. Everything you wanted. All kinds of meat, mashed potatoes, peas, corn, cakes, pies and ice cream. I ate and ate and ate. Then in a strange camp I got so sick in my bunk, I literally couldn't talk or move and I wouldn't have known where the sick bay was anyway. I must have finally fallen asleep and in the morning after visiting the men's room I was just fine.

I was sent home to Dubuque, IA. I arrived at Santa Ana, California on August 22, 1945. You needed 72 points for an honorable discharge. As I recall it was five points for each medal and points for state side service and overseas service. I came up with the 72 points and received my honorable discharge on October 27, 1945.

Upon discharge, Tony Helling, a fellow Dubuquer and I teamed up going home and we stopped to see his brother in California and went onto Chicago by train. In Chicago the hotels were filled up and we finally spotted a sign, "Free Rooms for Service Men". I didn't have any bags, but Tony did and the man behind the counter took them and put them behind the counter.

The next morning we got up early because we had to catch a train to Dubuque. The man said, "You can't leave now you have to stay for the religious service." Tony argued with the man but he wouldn't give in and give him his bags. Finally Tony went around the counter and just grabbed his baggage and we left.

It was a great feeling to hop on the train and get to our final stop, Dubuque. After the war there were times I reflected on the part I had in the destruction of Japan. I do feel remorse at times at the thought of the thousands and thousands of American lives lost and the incredible suffering of the Japanese people. However I knew it was them or us. It was something that had to be done. I truly hope that someday, somehow there is a peace in the world. In 1997, the last operational B-29, Fife, was displayed in my hometown, Dubuque, Iowa.

Z-48 "Million Dollar Baby" flew our 34th mission.

The Enola Gay is seen here after dropping the first atom bomb on Hiroshima on August 6, 1945.

"What have we done?"

Mushroom cloud above Hiroshima.

The B-29 "Bockscar" dropped the second atomic bomb
on Nagasaki on August 9, 1945.

Z-53, the "Ancient Mariner" unloading on Japan.

COMPARISON OF ATOMIC BOMB ATTACKS WITH OTHER BOMBINGS

Target (Average of 93 Attacks on Cities)	Hiroshima	Nagasaki	Tokyo Fire Raid
Dead/Missing	70,000–80,000	35,000–40,000	83,000
Wounded	70,000	40,000	102,000
Population Density	35,000 per sq mile	65,000 per sq mile	130,000 per sq mile
Total Casualties	140,000–150,000	75,000–80,000	185,000
Area Destroyed	4.7 sq miles	1.8 sq miles	15.8 sq mile
Attacking Platform	1 B-29	1 B-29	334 B-29s
Weapon(s)	'Tall Boy' 15,000 kiloton	'Fat Man' 22,000 kiloton	1667 tons

Incredible destruction.

I couldn't fit into my uniform at age 76.

Decorations awarded.

Japanese Foreign Minister Mamora Shigemitsu signs the surrender documents on board the USS Missouri on September 2, 1945.

"Fifi" the last operational B-29, displayed at the Dubuque
Municipal Airport in 1997.

At the Dubuque Municipal Airport was: (l-r) Joe Stieber, lucky me, and "Spook" Maloney. Joe had his foot blown off when stepping on a land mine in Normandy. "Spook" in the 8th Air Force was shot down over Germany and became a prisoner of war.

Veteran's Memorial, Dubuque, Iowa. In picture
Number 2 son, Steve, and me.

A Look Into The Years After WWII

River Gambling Boat

This was a part-time job I had on the Dubuque Casino Belle as a teller-cashier. Many times I worked with a black college student, Bernard. When I came back from a break he would say, "Wow, you just missed a really beautiful girl, she showed a lot of interest in you. Too bad! Ooh La La!" Then when he came back from a break I would say, "There were two gorgeous chicks here asking about you, even wanted me to give them your phone number."

A casino player asked Bernard, "Where is there a good dollar machine to play?" Bernard pointed and said, "That one". He didn't know a good machine from a poor one! The guy won; gave Bernard a tip and said, "Is there another one?" Again Bernard pointed to one and the guy won on that one too, and again gave Bernard a tip! This happened four times in a row, I couldn't believe it! The guy left happy.

Iowa Driver's License Examiner

I worked as an examiner at age 23 full time giving driving tests, eye tests, and patrolling on holidays, both in West Union and Sioux City, Iowa. The eye test was for distance. Some people could not pass it and were told to go to an eye doctor and get glasses. Many went to the drug store instead and bought reading glasses, which didn't work, they needed prescription glasses.

After all these years, I still know the letters, TPEOLF OLFTPE LFEOTP. I would tell them to read the letters and some tried to pronounce the words!

One wintry day there was a layer of ice on the highway, but it was a nice day with the sun shining. I was going from West Union, to Elkader, Iowa. A few miles out of town the ice started to melt and the highway became very slick! I approached a mile long downhill at about 10 MPH and started down. There was a car ahead of me about 30 yards. I put the patrol car in second gear to slow down but kept the same speed. I tried touching the brakes, still the same speed, and I was catching up to the car in front of me.

There was a huge drop off to the side of the highway so I couldn't attempt to pull off. I started honking the horn, the guy couldn't hear me or had decided not to go any faster. I turned on my siren, he still wouldn't go any faster. Finally I caught up to him and we hooked bumpers and we slid all the way down to the bottom of the hill. He said he tried but he couldn't go any faster!

The Big Big Man

I worked as a security guard at the Kennedy Mall, a part-time job. I opened and locked the mall, kept kids from running on the escalator, sitting on the floor and misbehaving in general. Also, I had to jimmy open locked cars when people locked themselves out.

One day, Harry Bemis, chief guard, who was a rugged individual, came to me and said, "There is a man in the mall about 350 pounds, he's been here before causing trouble and he is always belligerent and will fight. I need some help to get him out of the mall."

This was an experience I hadn't expected. We looked all around the mall but couldn't find him. Harry said, "Forget it, I guess he left the mall".

Can you believe it? After all these years I am still in one piece. Do you think I still have an angel on my shoulder?? I do!

I hope you have found this true story interesting, educational and entertaining.

On January 28, 1950, I married my beautiful wife Helen. We had five children; Blake, Steve, Gail, Dave, and Don, and at this time there is also ten grandchildren and five great grandchildren. We were blessed with a wonderful family. After fifty nine years of marriage sadly, very sadly, my wife passed away at the age of 82 on April 15, 2009. She was the best of the best. I miss her every day.

Kennedy Mall Guard.

Teller Cashier on the Dubuque Casino Belle

D. ..ers Examinations

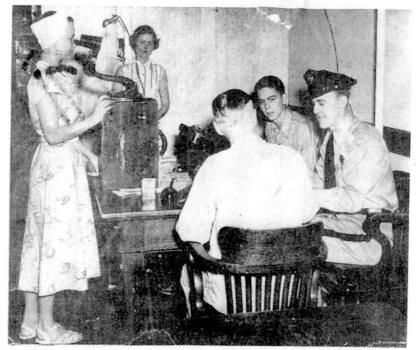

DRIVER'S LICENSE EXAMINATIONS have been conducted in the various counties of Iowa for the past two years under the Birthday Licen..e plan. The program went into effect in July, 1948. All driver's licenses must be renewed every two years within the 30 day period before the automobile operator's birthday. Chauffer's licenses must be renewed every year.

The day the above photo was taken in the ground floor corridor of the Winneshiek courthouse, 39 driver's licenses and 27 chauffer's licenses were issued or renewed. Patrolman Ed Heiberger presently of West Union is in charge of the examinations. Kenneth Light (seated on patrolman's right) is helping with the program during the summer as a clerk. He is attending Cornell college at Mt. Vernon. Carl Jacobson of Decorah (seated) is taking his driving exam, while Mrs. David Holman of Waukon takes the eye test. Marilyn Stabo of Decorah (in background) also awaits her driver's examination. Examinations are conducted every Thursday at the courthouse.

On January 28, 1950, the luckiest day of my life,
Helen E. Burds, became Mrs. Edward F. Heiberger.

LORAS COLLEGE
Commencement
May 11, 1980

Happy Graduate with wife, Helen. Graduated with
a B.A. degree at age 54.

Brother Ray, Mom, and I.

Bertille, me, Laura, Ray and Anna Mae. Anna Mae
and I are the only survivors.

An old picture I found of my dad. Dad and Mom loved horses.

(l-r) Dave, Don, Gail, me, Blake and Steve.

Above is Helen and me in 2003
celebrating our 53rd wedding anniversary.

FINIS